MW00425829

7

TRAITS OF A "TEACHER WITH A PURPOSE!"

© 2018 by Jahkari H. Taylor

All rights reserved. No portion of this book may be reproduced, stored in a retrieval system, or transmitted in any form or by any means—electronic, mechanical, photocopy, recording, scanning, or other – except for brief quotations without permission of the publisher.

1. Teacher 2. Education. I Title. II. Title: 7 Traits of a "Teacher with a Purpose!"

To obtain permission(s) to use material from this work, please submit a written request to jtwithapurpose@gmail.com

PURPOSE
PUSHERS

Printed in the United States of America.

1

7

Traits Of A

"Teacher With A Purpose!"

Jahkari Taylor

Relational Teaching
Connection is the Key!

Jahkari H. Taylor

Becoming One Flesh

Timeless Principles to Bless Your Marriage

Jahkari H. Taylor

Available @ www.purposepushers.com or Amazon.

Dedication

This book is dedicated to everyone in the field of education. To substitutes, custodians, cafeteria workers, bus drivers, paraprofessionals, school nurses, librarians, technology specialists, teachers, guidance counselors, school social workers, principals, professors, and all others; this book is dedicated to you.

You are all "Educators with a Purpose." No matter what role you play in the lives of young people, you are significant and necessary! You make a difference every day, and I truly thank God for you. Continue to stay strong, keep speaking life into children, and never give up!

Acknowledgments

First and foremost, I must acknowledge my Lord and Savior, Jesus Christ. He is the one who gives me the strength to teach with conviction and compassion, day in and day out. I would not be 1% of the man that I am today if you had not come into my life. Thank you for modeling what it means to be a "Teacher with a Purpose."

To my amazing and beautiful wife, Shalise – You are an exceptional educator, a wonderful wife, and a nurturing mother. As long as I have you by my side, I know that everything will be just fine. Thank you for your unconditional love and unwavering support. I love you to life!

To my loving mother, Beverly – You have instilled in me the values of hard work, respect, and determination. I am blessed to be your son. I love you.

To my tribe: Jahkari, Jaden, Jayla, Josiah, and Jyra – I love you all dearly. You all challenge me to be the best teacher and father that I can be, and you continue to remind me that educators still have a great deal to learn from children. I love and appreciate you all.

To the life-changing teachers who inspired me to pursue a career in the field of education: Mr. Boone, Mrs. Bookman, Prof. Prudhomme, and Dr. Andrejco – Thank you for seeing the potential that I could not see and thank you for believing in me.

To all my colleagues throughout my professional career – I just want to say thank you. Every discussion and nugget of wisdom you have given me has shaped me in some way. Keep striving to be "Teachers with a Purpose!" The world needs what you have to offer.

Table of Contents

Introduction: "Teachers Matter the Most" 10

Trait #1 - "Understanding" 16

Conclusion: Summarizing "Understanding" 25

Reflection, Response, and Affirmation 28

Trait #2 - "Empathy" 30

Conclusion: Summarizing "Empathy" 36

Reflection, Response, and Affirmation 40

Trait #3 - "Forgiveness" 42

Conclusion: Summarizing "Forgiveness" 51

Reflection, Response, and Affirmation 54

Trait #4 - "Resilience" 56

Conclusion: Summarizing "Resilience" 61

Reflection, Response, and Affirmation 64

Trait #5 - "Encouragement" 66

Conclusion: Summarizing "Encouragement" 73

Reflection, Response, and Affirmation 74

Trait #6 - "Hope" 76

Conclusion: Summarizing "Hopefulness" 80

Reflection, Response, and Affirmation 84

Trait #7 - "Relational" 86

Conclusion: Summarizing "Relational" 91

Reflection, Response, and Affirmation 92

Striving to be a "Teacher with A Purpose!" 94

Reflection, Response, and Affirmation 96

Meet the Author..98

References..100

Although class size, district funding, parental involvement, and a host of other factors contribute to student achievement, many studies acknowledge that teachers are the single-most influential school-related factor to student achievement (Cawelti, 1999; Stronge & Tucker, 2000).[i]

> *"Everyone who remembers his own education remembers teachers, not methods and techniques. The teacher is the heart of the educational system.*
> — *Sidney Hook*

To put it plainly, teachers matter the most. Even if a failing school went out to hire Joe Clark from the movie *Lean on Me* as their principal, the school would not move in the direction of success until quality teachers are hired or developed. Districts can invest in research-based programs to close the achievement gaps or purchase the latest technology to integrate into classrooms. Still, if they fail to hire, develop, and retain good teachers, nothing will matter. The reality is there is simply no substitute for teacher effectiveness.

"Teachers with a Purpose"

For this reason, I have set out to write a book that highlights seven traits of highly effective teachers. I refer to these teachers as "Teachers with a Purpose." In my opinion, Teachers with a Purpose are much more than ordinary teachers. They are life-changing educators who positively affect every student who enters their classroom. These are the type of teachers who are unforgettable. No matter how much time passes and no matter how old students become, they will always remember, Teachers with a Purpose.

Yet, it is not merely their attention to pedagogical best-practices that makes these educators unforgettable. Neither is it just their ability to help young people perform at high levels on summative assessments. Yes, they possess a personal zeal to align instruction and assessments with the curriculum framework to ensure they provide their students with the best instruction possible, but this is not what sets them apart from the rest. What sets Teachers with a Purpose apart from all others is not the content of their subject area, but rather the content of their character.

They are genuinely good people who truly have a heart filled with love and compassion. They stand, without wavering, on the fundamental truth that all students can learn and succeed. This truth allows them to look beyond

11

stereotypes and stigmas attached to students' socio-economic status, race, and family background to see the God-given potential in every child. To put it in laymen's terms, Teachers with a Purpose see things differently, including their occupation. They embrace a unique perception of the teaching profession. They tend to view their occupation through the lens of purpose, which means they do not see teaching as a *job*, but rather their life's *calling*.

These educators put every fiber of their being into a profession that pays modest wages, which is an extremely rare thing to do in a society driven by the desire to accumulate wealth by any means necessary. This is precisely why Teachers with a Purpose are as unique as the traits they embody. Like Haley's Comet, they do not come around often, but when they do, they leave a life-altering mark on their students. They do more than impact students for a school year; they impact students for a lifetime.

Many students recall that one special teacher who they would consider to be a Teacher with a Purpose. The one who knew how to inspire students to dream big. The one who went above and beyond to ensure that students felt capable, connected, and cared for in an atmosphere of love. The one who believed in students when students didn't

12

believe in themselves. Do you remember that one educator who made you feel like you could do something great in this world? As we take time to reminisce about the life-altering educators we have had throughout our own lives, we realize that every child deserves a life-altering educator, a Teacher with a Purpose.

Teachers with a Purpose – (noun)
Educators who "Know their WHY!" They believe in the life-changing power of education, and they are fully aware of their role in the lives of young people. These inspiring educators possess the character, values, and beliefs that are necessary to effectively teach students from all walks of life.

Developing "Teachers with a Purpose"

While some teachers may be able to enter the field of education and immediately be deemed as Teachers with a Purpose, most will have to develop the defining traits over time. I believe the future of the American educational system rests upon its ability to cultivate and develop these traits in every educator. Without a game-changing difference maker in every classroom, some students will not succeed in school. Many students will enter classrooms utterly burdened by life challenges that hinder their ability to achieve academic success. These students may perform below their potential for years until they encounter Teachers with a Purpose. This is because Teachers with a Purpose have a unique ability to connect with students in a way that empowers them to achieve despite their personal challenges.

Throughout this book, I intend to highlight seven traits that I believe characterize Teachers with a Purpose. These special traits are *character traits* that must take root in the heart of the educator. By no means am I saying these traits are exhaustive for being a highly effective educator, but I am saying I believe it will be difficult to be considered highly effective without these traits. If nothing else, I hope to spur a dialogue about professional development that will help educators embrace a mindset that welcomes personal growth in the teaching profession. Let's identify the *7 Traits of "Teachers with a Purpose!"*

Trait #1 - "Understanding"

In 1820, Thomas Jefferson wrote a letter in favor of the establishment of a state university in Virginia. He was a firm believer in the necessity of a good education and the importance of learning. He made

"The highest activity a human being can attain is learning for understanding, because to understand is to be free."
— Baruch Spinoza

it clear in his letter addressed to Joseph Cabell that "there can be no stronger proof that knowledge is power, and that ignorance is weakness."[ii] This truth articulated by Thomas Jefferson has been a staple of both ancient and modern societies, and it continues to be passed down from generation to generation. This truth is summarized by the famous proverb, which affirms, "Knowledge is power." While this is true, one could make the argument that the only thing more powerful than knowledge is *understanding*.

The ancient Hebrew concept of "understanding" refers to the application of wisdom and knowledge. In other words, understanding is what allows us to use wisdom properly. It is what gives us the ability to put knowledge into action. In other words, what good is it to possess knowledge that you do not know how to use? For example, all teachers know students need to learn, but not all teachers know how to ensure that all students are, in fact, learning in their classrooms. Likewise, all teachers know that if learning is to occur, behaviors in the classroom must be effectively managed. Yet, not all teachers know how to apply the knowledge that would lead to the successful implementation of effective classroom management procedures and practices. For these reasons, many students who matriculate through rigorous teacher preparation programs still feel insufficient as classroom teachers. Although they possess knowledge about the teaching profession, they still need "understanding." Not to mention, educators not only need to understand the critical components of the field of education but also the key components of the students they will teach. Moving beyond "knowing" about students to "understanding" students is essential to increasing student achievement. I believe seeking at least a general understanding of characteristics that define the students' generation will equip educators with valuable insight that can help them engage students in the learning process.

It is safe to say that most teachers were not born in the same generation as their students. This truth has many implications for the modern classroom. For one, students do not learn in the same way their teachers learn. They do not view school the same way their teachers view school, and they do not espouse the same values their teachers espouse. In the most general sense, students do not see the world the way their teachers see the world. However, this is not a bad thing. Intergenerational dialogue can be fascinating and informative. The issue is that it rarely occurs in classrooms.

In actuality, many students are likely to encounter a teacher who looks down on their entire generation as if they are all uninformed and uncivilized, yet every generation has strengths and weaknesses. Students certainly do not need someone to demean them because they were born during the 2000s, as opposed to being born during the 60s, 70s, or 80s. They do not need someone to make them feel bad because they are not "older, more mature, and experienced." They need someone to understand who they are, how they became that way, and what must be done to reach them. They need someone willing to invest time in

learning about the unique characteristics of their
generation.

What does the research say?

If you are a part of the teaching force today, you
will be working with students who are categorized as
"Millennials or GenZ" (2001-Present).[iii] I believe there are
five characteristics that describe modern students that all
educators should seek to understand. These five
characteristics may manifest themselves in the learning
environment in many ways, but teachers who understand
them will undoubtedly be better equipped to increase
student achievement.

1. "Fun"

If you envision yourself standing behind a desk,
lecturing a group of well-behaved students as they sit
quietly in their chairs for 40-90 minutes, you are in for a
rude awakening. This modern generation of students
believe in their hearts that school is a place to have a good
time. They want to have fun. This does not mean they do
not welcome learning, and this does not mean they reject
rules and order. Contrary to popular belief, most students
want structure, and they do not mind rules. They are also

willing to meet the high expectations set by the staff. However, they still want an opportunity to enjoy the learning environment. In the simplest terms, students don't want to be bored. In fact, if they sense boredom in school, they will immediately begin to create their own fun at the expense of rules, order, and the sanity of their teachers. What this means is teachers of today must be dynamic communicators who can keep students engaged in the learning process for the duration of a class period. In addition, teachers must use creativity to foster interaction within the classroom. Therefore, it should not be abnormal to bring academic games into the teaching and learning experience. Students expect to have fun!

2. "Extremely Tech-Savvy"

Teachers should also understand that this generation of students was pretty much born with smartphones, tablets, and laptops in their hands. They have been accustomed to staring at some type of screen since their inception. Therefore, using technology is not only an excellent way to practice skills and introduce new concepts, but it is also a "fun" way to engage students in the learning process. Yet, some teachers take it upon themselves to completely ban screens or limit student access to them for whatever reasons. When "screens" are neglected from the curriculum, student disengagement is likely to ensue. This is because this generation of students feel as if they cannot live without some type of "screen."

As an Instructional Coach, I have witnessed firsthand the perils of teaching without technology integration. Student engagement usually dwindles, student achievement tends to decrease, and teacher frustration ultimately flies off the chart. This occurs because bored students often become inattentive, fidgety, and disruptive. These issues can be addressed by incorporating "screens" into the lesson. With an understanding of why technology integration is essential for this generation, educators can equip themselves with the tools needed to increase engagement in schools. I encourage educators to pursue professional development on how to integrate technology best to meet the unique needs of this generation.

3. "Family Oriented"

Students of today are also considered to be "family oriented." To some, this may seem like a surprising sentiment. However, it speaks to their extreme need for community validation. They crave acceptance, belonging, and cooperation, and they want to feel as if they are an integral part of something much bigger than themselves. In addition, they want their families to be involved in their education. I once surveyed over 800 students who attended a diverse Title 1 middle school, where over 90% of the students received free or reduced lunch. In the survey, I asked the students if they expected their parents to motivate them in school, and over 90% indicated that they expected their parents to motivate them more than their teachers. I believe this speaks to the role parental involvement must play in the success of this new generation of students. It will be incumbent upon the educational system to bridge the gap between schools and the communities they serve. I personally believe it should be a requirement for educators to call parents/guardians during the first two weeks of school, at least once, just to introduce themselves and express their goals for the class at large. This would help facilitate parental involvement and help parents develop a more positive perception of classroom teachers. If the parent only speaks with educators when children exhibit problematic behaviors, relational trust will be difficult to establish. This will ultimately hinder student achievement, especially since most students expect their parents to be involved in the educational process.

4. "Individualistic but Group-Oriented"

Although students are often characterized as selfish and self-centered (which they are), they are also regarded as "team-players" who enjoy working in groups. [iv] This bodes well in the modern classroom with students of varying abilities and interests. By using project-based assessments that allow students to work in pairs or small groups, teachers will meet students' *group-oriented* and social-emotional needs. Additionally, from an instructional perspective, grouping students can also set the stage for 100% engagement in the learning environment. Not to mention, it will help students develop the collaborative skills needed to function in the competitive, team-oriented post-secondary world. Students must be provided with opportunities to develop these invaluable skills. As educators teach with the end in mind, they will be more inclined to put students in the best position to be contributing members of a globalized society, which means incorporating opportunities to develop skills in collaboration and teamwork.

5. "Sociability"

According to the Oxford dictionary, "sociability" refers to "the quality of being social." This trait, by far, captures the true identity of the modern student. They are social butterflies who are in love with social media and the attention they can gain from it. This is why they enthusiastically seek Instagram followers. It's *sociability*! While it is clear that students crave attention from their age-group peers, they also want attention from adults. Even when students appear to be introverted by nature, they still want to be acknowledged and affirmed by those around them. Sometimes this trait can be an asset, and at other times it can be a liability. Students' sociability tends to make them extremely susceptible to peer influence.

One disadvantage of a highly social generation is the fact that many young people can become self-conscious and anxious about what others say and think about them. In some extreme cases, young people can feel pressured to join gangs, engage in bullying behaviors, or experiment with self-injurious behaviors, such as sexual promiscuity or drugs. Educators must seek to understand the "sociability" factor that drives students of today. By understanding it, schools can prepare to address it from a more positive and constructive angle. For example, implementing youth mentoring programs, peer tutoring, and social clubs can help students meet their social needs within appropriate boundaries.

Conclusion: Summarizing "Understanding"

I believe Teachers with a Purpose, first and foremost, must seek to *understand* children. They must seek to understand who children are at their core and how they became that way. For this reason, I encourage every educator to become a "student of students." I believe once this foundation is laid, everything can be built upon it. Yet, when teachers reject the notion that they should learn just as much from their students as their students are expected to learn from them, I believe professional growth is doomed. Teachers must invest time in learning about the generation they seek to serve and inspire. Without knowledge of the students' generation and an understanding of how to meet their unique needs, educators will not be able to help students achieve to their potential.

> *"Students need teachers who understand them. They do not need someone who will look down upon them as if they are inferior and uncivilized beings who need to be tamed."*

Understanding students' generational characteristics is just one piece to the puzzle. Yet, I believe it is a crucial prerequisite to personalizing learning. How can you meet students' needs if you fail to understand those needs? How can you create a bridge that leads to academic success if you fail to pinpoint where students are coming from? Seeking to understand the characteristics of a generation may give you the most "bang for your buck" in terms of where to start the bridge building process. Educators will still need to develop meaningful relationships with students on a personal level, but at least understanding their generational characteristics will give educators a starting point. There's no need to go into the process blindly with no prior knowledge of general characteristics that define students.

There's Much to *Understand*

Although this chapter focused specifically on understanding the generational needs of your students, I still want to encourage all Teachers with a Purpose to understand the following:

1. how to build relationships with students of varying racial, cultural, and socioeconomic backgrounds,
2. how to motivate and inspire students to put forth their best efforts in the classroom,
3. how to unpack the curriculum framework to ensure instruction addresses the essential skills,
4. how to deliver innovative lessons that will keep students fully engaged and on-task,

5. how to apply effective behavioral management strategies to ensure the learning environment is safe and orderly,

6. how to work with colleagues collaboratively,

7. how to contribute to professional learning communities,

8. how to demonstrate the basics of professionalism,

9. how to develop your yearly professional development plan to direct your personal growth,

10. how to overcome teacher burnout, which is the cause of a mass exodus in the field of education,

11. and much more!

Reflection, Response, and Affirmation
Trait #1 - "Understanding"

"Understanding" Students

- Are you the type of person who seeks to "understand" before drawing conclusions, or do you allow your personal life experiences to lead your approach to students? *Proverbs 4:7 states, "Wisdom is the principal thing; therefore, get wisdom. And in all your getting, get understanding."*

- Are you aware of the role your personal views play in helping or hurting your understanding of the generation in which you teach? *We all have individual biases we bring into the classroom.*

- Do you sometimes embrace a culture that belittles students because their entire generation is "lazy and entitled?" *Engaging in honest reflection will undoubtedly help your professional growth.*

- What will you do to seek an understanding of your students' interests, needs, and views about education? (Tweet your response to @purposepushers using the hashtag #iunderstand.)

• Will you accept the challenge of reaching your students' generation by making your classroom and lesson plans more "fun," "tech-savvy," "family-oriented," "individualistic but group-oriented," and "socially engaging?" *(Culturally-responsive practices are mandatory!)*

"Understanding" Adults

• How might you apply the concept of "understanding" to your interactions with adults? *Understanding adults is usually more taxing and more complicated than understanding children.*

Affirmation: "I am a Teacher with a Purpose"

• "I am expected to be a difference maker in my profession, and I fully understand my influence has the potential to impact children as well as adults. I must seek to model an understanding attitude at all times."

Trait #2 - "Empathy"

According to the Oxford dictionary, "Empathy" is defined as "the ability to understand and share the feelings of another." It is the capacity to put yourself in someone else's situation and consider life from their perspective as if you experienced what they have experienced. As a teacher, empathy

"Empathy is the most mysterious transaction that the human soul can have, and it's accessible to all of us, but we have to give ourselves the opportunity to identify, to plunge ourselves in a story where we see the world from the bottom up or through another's eyes or heart."
— *Sue Monk Kidd*

may be the most necessary trait required to help all students achieve academic excellence. Specifically, this is because some students will enter the classroom carrying a tremendous load of "invisible baggage." *Invisible baggage refers to the psychological and social-emotional burdens that impede academic achievement.* These burdens are usually hidden from plain sight. All students carry invisible baggage, and most will never expose their baggage to educators until relational trust has been established.

Invisible baggage can be caused by traumatic life experiences, familial dysfunction, emotional distress, poverty, and a host of other environmental influences that are beyond the students' control. For example, I have worked with students who inherited generational poverty and home environments that did not place a high value on education. I have worked with students who were abandoned by their biological parents and placed in foster care systems. I have also worked with students who have experienced extreme neglect and physical abuse. All these situations can place a heavy emotional load on students, causing them to become insecure, apathetic, or emotionally unstable. In addition, invisible baggage tends to cause students to shift their pursuit of academic success to the bottom of their priority list.

Teachers must always be mindful of the fact that students did not willfully choose to experience adversities that create invisible baggage. They did not sign up for a stressful life. Unfortunately for students, they can inherit a dysfunctional upbringing from adults who were entrusted to care for them. In many cases, the dysfunction leads to psychological trauma that ends up being carried into the classrooms. As I have previously stated, this invisible baggage can weigh on a student's psyche, causing anxieties and insecurities that hinder academic achievement. Yet, the good news for students is one empathetic teacher who is willing to listen and give students a voice, without judgment or condemnation, maybe all they need to begin the process of self-discovery. This is required if students are to move from an identity of anger and resentment toward purpose and fulfillment. Teachers with a Purpose can facilitate this transition, which is why they are necessary for every school across the country.

Naturally, being empathetic requires understanding. Think about it… How can a teacher demonstrate empathy toward a student they don't understand? Once teachers develop an understanding of their students and where their students come from, they will have met the prerequisite for demonstrating empathy. In the modern school system, teachers are likely to encounter countless students who are weighed down by the invisible baggage they carry. In most cases, students who carry invisible baggage will fail to achieve at their academic potential unless they encounter an empathetic Teacher with a Purpose who puts forth a concerted effort to help them succeed.

What does the research say?

One massive reason why all teachers must demonstrate empathy is because of the detrimental impact poverty has on student achievement. According to the US Census Bureau (2016), over 40 million Americans are

living in poverty, and of those, over 13 million are kids.[v]
This means throughout a teacher's lifetime; they are likely
to engage thousands of students who carry the invisible
baggage caused by the adverse impact of poverty. With
this being the case, teachers must seek an understanding of
poverty and the risk factors that accompany it. The diagram
below shows a few risk factors associated with poverty and
to what extent those factors negatively impact students'
academic achievement.

Poverty's Environmental Risk Factors and Academic Achievement

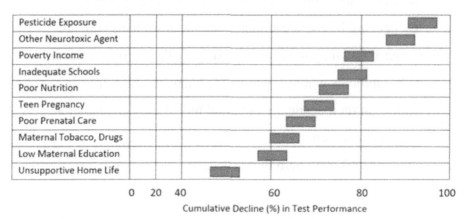

Cumulative Decline (%) in Test Performance

Source: Adapted from "Environmental Toxicants and Developmental Disabilities: A Challenge for Psychologists" by S. M. Koger, T. Schettler, and B. Weiss. 2005, *American Psychologist* 60(3), pp.252.

The diagram above indicates the adverse impact of poverty
and risk factors associated with it. These factors harm

student achievement. Therefore, it is imperative to equip all teachers with the tools they will need to work with impoverished students. Before providing specific strategies, teachers need to first develop at least a broad awareness of poverty's impact on brain development and behavior.

Poverty's Impact on Brain Development

In 2016, Duke University published an article titled, "How Living in Poverty Affects Children's Brain Development." According to the article, the "stress of living in poverty affects children's brains in ways that are similar to the effects from abuse."[vi] Researchers from the University of Wisconsin-Madison have also expressed a similar sentiment. After examining over 800 brain scans of children whose ages ranged from 4-17, they concluded that brain growth and educational achievement are adversely impacted by the stress caused by poverty.[vii] These researchers believe the specific areas of the brain which regulate problem solving, memory, attention, judgment, emotion, and language are all hindered by factors related to and subsequently caused by poverty. Malnutrition, limited access to health care, exposure to environmental toxins, violence, and income inequities were all cited as factors that may accompany poverty and hinder brain development and learning.[viii]

Poverty's Impact on Behavior

Scientists have noted the adverse impact poverty has on brain development but also behavior. At the International Convention of Psychological Science held in Amsterdam, four scientists demonstrated the suppressing impact poverty has on cognitive development, attention, and executive functioning.[ix] According to *Understood.org*, executive functioning refers to the following skills:

1. Paying attention
2. Organizing and planning
3. Initiating tasks and staying focused on them
4. Regulating emotions
5. Self-monitoring and self-control.[x]

This research challenges many of the stigmas and stereotypes associated with impoverished students. Maybe impoverished students are not always intentionally trying to be disorganized, defiant, disruptive, and disrespectful. Some of their behavior could very well be attributed to or exacerbated by neurological deficits caused by long-term stress-induced by poverty. Whether individuals agree with the research or not, the reality is educators must consider the detrimental impact poverty may have on their students. Once this occurs, teachers will have the choice to respond with the type of empathy needed to teach replacement behaviors, character development, and organizational skills that can curtail the adverse impact of poverty.

Conclusion: Summarizing "Empathy"

Teachers with a Purpose, above all else, are expected to care. They are expected to be empathetic and compassionate toward students. Empathetic teachers will undoubtedly give themselves the best chance of helping the neediest learners. This is because empathy will cause a person to go above and beyond to alleviate the

"Yet, the good news for students is one empathetic teacher who is willing to listen and give students a voice, without judgement or condemnation, may be all they need to begin the process of self-discovery that ultimately places them on the road to high academic achievement."

distress or misfortune of another. Meaning, educators who understand the invisible baggage carried by students will seek professional development to enhance their teaching capacity to ensure they are equipped to help all students succeed. It should not matter if students are reared in dysfunctional families, homes that undermine the importance of education, or environments that are riddled with violence, they should still have equitable access to academic achievement. Teachers with a Purpose embrace this mentality wholeheartedly. They understand their purpose as one who has the potential to transform lives in the context of the classroom or school system.

Empathy is not only needed to inspire growth in terms of student success, but it's also necessary to drive growth in terms of educator professional development. In many cases, empathetic educators will be more likely to engage in research because they care about their ability to reach the seemingly "unreachable." Discovering the best practices and strategies for improving the academic outcomes of impoverished students requires a diligent work ethic. Only one who is willing to invest in themselves through the careful excavation of scholarly articles and existing literature will discover the tools needed to be a true change agent in the classroom. When teachers invest in their skills, they can equip themselves with the strategies needed to curb poverty's debilitating impact on student achievement. Poverty should not be a deal breaker for student success. Even if students enter classrooms weighed down by the invisible baggage caused by poverty, they should be given the best chance to succeed. An empathetic Teacher with a Purpose will ensure that this occurs.

Here are (3) actions steps schools can take to develop empathetic Teachers with a Purpose who are aware of the adverse impact poverty has on students:

1. **Professional Development** – Teachers will not stand a chance at providing impoverished students with equitable access to academic success without knowledge and strategies for what works for impoverished students and why. Professional development can come in the form of a school-wide book assignment, sending staff to a workshop or conference, or disseminating articles within the building. No matter which approach is taken, one thing is true: raising educator awareness of the impact of poverty on student achievement and behavior is necessary to improve educational outcomes for impoverished students.

2. **Motivational Speaker** – Trending in the educational system is the concept of dynamic motivational speakers. Motivational speakers can provide a jolt of inspiration to a staff that feels depleted, drained, and burnt out. Since this

occupation is trending, schools must meticulously vet potential candidates. Nevertheless, motivational speakers who specifically have overcome the crippling effects of poverty can help give educators hope as they consider what they must do to help their students succeed.

3. **Foster an Empathetic Climate** – Undoubtedly, schools that seek to develop an empathetic and caring environment will be best suited to confront the invisible baggage that impoverished students bring into the school environment. Use research to confront popular stereotypes staff members may embrace about impoverished individuals. Also, remain radically optimistic and stand on the conviction that all people can grow. This includes students who are adversely impacted by poverty and adults who are crippled by prejudices.

Reflection, Response, and Affirmation
Trait #2 - "Empathy"

"Empathy" for Students

- What can an educator do personally to demonstrate empathy in the classroom? (Tweet your response to @purposepushers using the hashtag #EducatorEmpathy.)

- On a scale from 1 to 10, (1 meaning "not that important" to 10 meaning "extremely important"), where would you rank educator "empathy?"

- Do you offer students an opportunity to express their feelings in class via journals or discussions that engage their emotional well-being? *Giving students a voice validates their humanity and is a vital tool in the relationship-building process.*

- Choose one of the following that best describes yourself:

  1. "I am aware of some of the struggles people have in the world."

  2. "Sometimes, I cry when I hear stories about suffering."

  3. "I volunteer to serve people less fortunate than myself."

• Will you accept the challenge of learning about the impact poverty may have on your students? *Growth equals happiness!*

Suggested Reading:
Poor Students, Rich Teaching: Mindsets for Change (Data-Driven Strategies for Overcoming Student Poverty and Adversity in the Classroom to Increase Student Success) by Eric Jensen

"Empathy" for Adults

• How might you apply the concept of "empathy" to your interactions with adults? *Empathy is a trait of strong character. When it is lacking, a person can easily become bitter, apathetic, and unhelpful. Children are not the only people who need empathy. Our world needs more empathetic people.*

Affirmation: "I am a Teacher with a Purpose"

• "I will embrace the responsibility to demonstrate empathy in my classroom, in my school, and my community. I will commit to being the positive change I desire to see in my world by modeling the empathy I expect from others."

Trait #3 - "Forgiveness"

A wise man once said, "If two people remain in close proximity to one another over an extended period, conflict will certainly occur."

> *"The weak can never forgive. Forgiveness is an attribute of the strong."*
> — *Mahatma Gandhi*

Since schools are places where hundreds of people occupy the same space, I guess educators should expect to experience one hundred times the conflict of an average person. For teachers, conflict is a normal part of the job. There will obviously be times when educators must confront students about their academic and/or behavioral performance in school. There will also be times when students confront educators because of disagreements students may have. The occurrence of conflict is not always problematic. In fact, as schools equip students with the self-advocacy skills needed for life in the post-secondary arena, students will become much more vocal and much more confrontational.

The downside to confrontation in the educational system lies in the emotional damage that can result from the conflict. When students feel embarrassed or offended, their desire to be confrontational may be fueled by anger, rage, or apathy. When this occurs, students may become disrespectful, noncompliant, or completely disengaged from the learning environment. On the other hand, when teachers feel embarrassed or offended by students, their emotions can also result in inappropriate behaviors. Sometimes these behaviors may manifest as sarcastic or belittling comments, and at other times it can manifest as frequently sending a student to the principal's office for minor issues that could be handled within the classroom. The reality is teachers and students are all humans with human emotions. Yet, the professional is expected to respond appropriately more frequently than the student. This means teachers must be the first to demonstrate and model forgiveness.

Forgiveness Requires Determination

According to the Oxford dictionary, *to forgive* is to "stop feeling angry or resentful toward (someone) for an offense, flaw, or mistake." If educators are expected to stop feeling angry or resentful toward people who offend them, they're most definitely going to need some help with this. This is because forgiveness is not as easy as grading papers. It is much more complex than differentiating instruction. Forgiveness requires a determined attitude to excuse the flaws, mistakes, and errors of others. Educators

43

will undoubtedly have numerous opportunities to practice forgiveness with students as well as staff members.

A Forgiving School?

In an article titled, "Forgiveness in the Workplace," author Michael Stone states, "One of the reasons this [forgiveness] is difficult at work is that our organizational and legal structures create cultural norms which do not support acts of forgiveness – someone (or something) is always to 'blame' – and if we let people 'off the hook,' there is a fear that this would be a signal that such behavior is condoned and it would undermine accountability; ultimately setting a bad example for other employees."[xi] Although Mr. Stone is not writing specifically about the field of education, I believe his point is well taken for educators. The educational system may not be constructed to endorse or promote forgiveness. A student who makes a mistake is more likely to be sent to the principal's office than to hear, "I forgive you." Likewise, an educator who makes a mistake is more likely to be "called to the carpet" for the mistake as opposed to hearing, "I forgive you." Maybe schools are not constructed to be institutions that promote and model forgiveness.

When teachers are offended by other teachers or other staff members, collaboration can be negatively impacted. Think about it… How often is an educator offended by another educator within the same department, team, or professional learning community? How does the offense impact collaboration and teamwork? How do you collaborate effectively with someone who has offended you or been the cause of your distrust? In many schools, effective teaming is hindered by past offenses, and poor collaboration is perpetuated by the inability to forgive. This issue happens more than we would like to acknowledge in schools and other places of employment.

"Offense and Forgiveness"

Forgiveness is certainly one of the most powerful traits of a Teacher with a Purpose. It is a trait that can impact an educator's emotional well-being for the better. From a psychological perspective, coping with stress and managing emotions effectively is one of the keys to happiness. This premise is no different for educators. Educators must learn to cope effectively with daily stressors while managing their emotions. On any given day, educators can deal with a tremendous amount of emotional stress. The teaching profession itself affords countless opportunities to be frustrated, disappointed, and/or offended. In fact, it is possible for educators to be offended by students, teachers, administrators, supervisors, and life situations outside of work (parenting, marriage, financial issues, etc.) all in the same day. Therefore, it is essential for teachers to use forgiveness as a tool to manage stress that comes from being offended.

When teachers are offended, joy can be replaced by anger, and happiness can be replaced by bitterness. These negative emotions can follow teachers into their classrooms, schools, and their homes. When this occurs, it ultimately takes a toll on the physical health and well-being of educators. In many cases, the emotional toll of being offended and carrying stress leads to teacher burnout. So for the sake of peace, emotional well-being, and career longevity, teachers must always be ready and willing to offer forgiveness.

> According to Michael Stone: *"The practice of forgiveness supports the development of organizational cultures where people feel free to take responsible risks, stop withholding their creativity, and demonstrate personal ownership and enthusiastic contribution. We can create greater internal harmony and healing by practicing the art of forgiveness, by using failures and unwanted situations to develop a culture of compassion and understanding, a place where people feel safe to express fully their natural genius and creativity, a place where they feel appreciated and experience a sense of joy and meaning from their work"* (Stone, 2002, p.279).

Clearly, all human beings must learn to let it go and let people off the hook. Teachers are no different. As I stated earlier, teachers will have countless opportunities to be offended, but each offense also presents an opportunity to master the art of forgiveness. I recall personal experiences in my classroom that taught me the power of forgiveness. During my first year of teaching, I had a new student named "Todd" (pseudonym) who transferred into my class from another school. The copious amount of paperwork that followed Todd indicated that he was certainly carrying a ton of invisible baggage. He was a 17-year-old white male with a troubled track record and a reputation that made teachers and principals quiver. At his previous school, Todd's teachers created a Behavioral Intervention Plan (BIP) to address the problematic behaviors he exhibited in school. Still, it did not lead to a decrease in Todd's disruptive outbursts.

When he arrived in my class for his first day at his new school, he was clearly apprehensive. He didn't know any of the students, which is probably why he was quiet for the greater part of the day. After a few days, he started to slowly come out of his shell. He tried to revert to some of the rude and disrespectful behaviors that were documented

47

in all the paperwork that transferred in from his previous school. When I confronted him about the rules and expectations of my classroom, he looked at me with a disturbed facial expression and yelled out, "You're a douchebag!" All my students immediately burst into hysterical laughter and began to stare at me to see how I would respond.

I am sure my response was not what any of my students anticipated because I, too, burst into hysterical laughter. Then I said, "That was a good joke, Todd, but inappropriate comments are not what we do in this class." Then I proceeded to teach my lesson for the day. At the end of the lesson, I walked over to Todd and asked him to remain in his seat, even after class dismissed so that I could speak with him privately. I knew I would have to remove the audience if Todd was going to receive anything I wanted to say to him. Once every student left, I approached Todd with a brand-new notebook and said, "This is my gift to you." He said, "What's this for?" I told him, "This notebook is for you to write down all of the inappropriate comments that come to your head. You cannot verbalize them in my class, but you can write them down in this notebook." He looked at me with the most curious and concerned face and said, "Ok." Then he went ahead to his next class.

Although not perfect, this situation could have easily been far worse. I could have responded impulsively to Todd's rude comments by sending him to the principal's office to show him who's the boss. I could have taken his comments personally and become frustrated and angered. However, I knew Todd, and I would have to coexist in my class if he was going to have any chance of graduating from high school. I knew I was his last chance. Therefore, I responded with forgiveness. I didn't have to verbally say, "I forgive you" because my actions spoke for me. Todd knew in his heart that I decided to *let it go* that day. I can honestly say that "douchebag" moment was the beginning of a great relationship between Todd and myself.

Model and Lead Forgiveness

Once Todd understood my rules, expectations, and my heart for helping all students succeed, he was never disrespectful or rude to me or anyone else in my class. As the year progressed, I often used weekly journals to engage Todd and the rest of my students in social-emotional learning, so they could become more mindful of their invisible baggage. Throughout that year, I learned a great

49

deal about Todd and how he became who he was. On one occasion, Todd expressed how his mother and father experienced vicious turmoil in their relationship for years until it ended in a bitter divorce. Although he was a young child when the divorce was finalized, he always felt as if he was just a pawn for financial gain. He believed his father didn't love him anymore, and he believed his mother only wanted physical custody of him because it gave her the ability to receive more spousal and child support. These factors caused Todd to be extremely resentful and rightfully, so; he felt unloved and abandoned by his own parents. I knew he needed to open his heart so he could extend forgiveness, but this would not be an easy task. Todd had so much emotional pain bottled up on the inside.

One day in my attempt to help Todd cope with life, I taught a lesson about "forgiveness." I had students copy the definition from the dictionary, and then I led them into a discussion about the pros and cons of forgiveness. They were instructed to explain a time when someone forgave them for something they did, while also acknowledging a time when they forgave someone else who offended them. Once every student shared their story, I shared my own personal story about the time when I called my father to offer forgiveness. As soon as I explained that I grew up in a single-parent home without my father, all my students were attentively clinging to my every word. (I believe this was the case because 100% of my students also came from a single-parent home, and they could definitely relate to my situation.) Nevertheless, I explained that my father was absent from my life. I told the class that "I did not want him to feel as if he could never be forgiven for his actions. I stated, "Sometimes children have to take the initiative to contact their parents to extend forgiveness. When you extend forgiveness, it gives you freedom and makes you feel better about yourself." That lesson about forgiveness was by far the most powerful lesson I had ever taught in my class up to that point. Although I am unsure if Todd ever extended forgiveness to his parents, I am happy with the fact that I was able to plant the seeds of forgiveness in his heart that day.

Conclusion: Summarizing "Forgiveness"

Teachers with a Purpose must be willing to demonstrate forgiveness at work.

"When you extend forgiveness, it gives you freedom and makes you feel better about yourself."

Harboring feelings of anger, resentment, and bitterness toward students or staff is counter-productive and self-defeating. It can create a prison cell of isolation that inhibits one's ability to collaborate or work in a team atmosphere. In fact, anyone who is unwilling to offer forgiveness is like a prisoner who locks himself in a cell and throws away the key to his own freedom. Therefore, forgiveness is a necessary life skill that all humans needs to develop. Teachers need to be especially aware of this because modeling forgiveness may give students the keys needed to set themselves free from invisible baggage that has been weighing them down emotionally and psychologically. I believe modeling and teaching students the significance of emotional stability is a necessary part of providing students with a quality education. Since students are inexperienced, cognitively underdeveloped, and desperately in need of direction, someone must step up and help them understand the importance of forgiveness. This is why Teachers with a Purpose are crucial to the field of education.

Remember, every opportunity to become angry, bitter, and resentful is also an opportunity to master the art of forgiveness. Do not choose to punish yourself by harboring unforgiveness in your heart. I encourage you to let go of any past offenses and free yourself to be the most effective educator you can be.

Reflection, Response, and Affirmation
Trait #3 - "Forgiveness"

"Forgiving" Students

- *Be honest with yourself:* Are you easily offended? Do you have a difficult time letting things go?
- Have you ever been truly offended by a student to the degree that you were literally angry with him or her?
- *Be honest...* Do you believe certain offenses are unforgivable?
- Will you accept the challenge of practicing forgiveness in your classroom, school, and in personal life outside of school?
- In your own opinion, think of one time you forgave someone. Let me know how it made you feel. (Tweet your response to @purposepushers using the hashtag #iForgive.)

"Forgiving" Adults

- Have you ever been offended by a colleague?
- Do you think it is more difficult to extend forgiveness to your colleagues as opposed to your students?

• How might you apply the concept of "forgiveness" to your interactions with adults in your school? *Do not imprison yourself by holding on to grudges against your coworkers or administrators.*

Affirmation: "I am a Teacher with a Purpose"

• "Although extending forgiveness is not an easy task, today I am making a commitment to letting go of all bitterness and resentment hidden in my heart. Life is too short to hold grudges that steal my peace, my happiness, and my joy. Therefore, today, I am choosing to let go and forgive."

Trait #4 - "Resilience"

In 2016, a teacher at an inner-city school in Richmond, Virginia, was recorded on a student's cell phone storming out

> *"A good school teaches you resilience - that ability to bounce back."*
> — Kate Reardon

of class, exclaiming, "I don't deserve it!"[xii] The teacher was visibly frustrated and emotionally exhausted. He had endured all that he could and finally reached his breaking point. He left the classroom and did not return that day. These instances of teachers feeling completely frustrated and overwhelmed are occurring all too often in schools across the United States. Obviously, educational leaders must do a better job attending to the emotional well-being of educators because stress may be pushing many qualified educators out of the classroom. One foundational discussion educational leaders may want to have with staff pertains to coping with stress and developing *resilience* in the workplace.

Resilience is the Remedy

Resilience is a trait that every person would benefit from developing, especially teachers. According to the Oxford dictionary, resilience is "the capacity to recover quickly from difficulties." Similar to Angela Duckworth's concept of "grit," which is generally defined as "a combination of passion and perseverance for a singularly important goal," resilience is also a trait that requires mental toughness."[xiii] However, I believe resilience requires an additional step. It is more like *"getting up from hardship,"* while grit seems to be more like *"pressing through hardship."* While both actions are beneficial traits to develop, getting up seems to require more energy and effort in comparison to pressing through. For example, if two boxers are beating each other bloody for nine consecutive rounds, they both must make a conscious decision to stay the course, press through, and keep fighting. Yet, if one of them gets knocked down, he or she must exert additional energy to get back up, press through, and keep fighting. I think this analogy paints a decent picture of what teacher resilience must look like. Each day, teachers must make a conscious decision to get up, press through, and keep fighting despite taking punches that will leave them feeling beat, battered, and bruised.

For this reason, Teachers with a Purpose must employ coping mechanisms that enhance their ability to be resilient. They must possess the ability to recover after getting knocked down or experiencing hardship. For teachers, hardship comes in many forms. It could look like a large group of students failing to demonstrate growth on state-sanctioned end of course assessments; it could look like student loan servicers calling to explain that your next month's payment will be one-third of your paycheck, or it could look like the loss of one of your beloved family members. Remember, educators are normal people with normal life experiences. The only difference is they are expected to show up to work, passionately teach a couple dozen kids, and conceal the "real struggles" they have going on outside of work. This is difficult for anyone, no matter the level of fortitude he or she possesses. Nevertheless, this is exactly why Teachers with a Purpose must learn to cope and be resilient.

What does the research say?

Resilience is a "centrally important construct in understanding how individuals respond to workplace stressors and appears to be a major determinant of whether or not certain unfavorable outcomes such as burnout, compassion fatigue, anxiety, or depression ensue"[xiv] (Rees, Breen, Cusack, and Hegney, 2015). No matter the occupation, professionals who possess the trait of resilience, are far more likely to manage job stress effectively and perform at a high level. Therefore, resilience should be among the top traits employers look for from their employees. The reality is all jobs are accompanied by stress. Employees will receive a paycheck, maybe some benefits, and possibly a migraine caused by job stress.

Job Stress

For simplicity sake, I refer to the stress caused by one's job as "job stress."[xv] Job stress, like all stress, can negatively impact a person's health and lead to a reduced performance on the job. When job stress worsens and goes unchecked, it can cause job "burnout." Burnout was first coined in the early 1970s by a psychologist named Herbert Freudenberger, who studied the concept of "staff burnout.[xvi] Freudenberger defined burnout as a "state of physical and emotional depletion resulting from conditions of work."[xvii] In the most general sense, it is sufficient to say burnout is caused by prolonged job stress that eventually turned into emotional exhaustion.

This concept of burnout is starting to become a popular term in the field of education under the alias of "teacher burnout." Yet, teacher burnout is not simply a buzzword without merit or credibility. According to

Cheryl Scott Williams (2011), "Research shows the teaching profession has the highest burnout rate of any public service job."[xviii] Some people may be shocked by this sentiment, but I am 99.9% sure teachers are not surprised. In fact, there is an educational cliché that can be heard throughout schools across the nation, namely "There is no stress like teacher stress." This phrase has a lot of truth to it because there are some stressors that are unique to the field of education. For example, on any given day, a teacher may be tasked with accomplishing a combination of the following:

- developing lesson plans that will maintain the attention of 30 students,
- motivating disengaged students to put forth their best effort on assessments,
- managing the classroom of students who demonstrate disrespectful behaviors,
- counseling students who may have endured traumatic life experiences,
- conferencing with demanding parents,
- collaborating with teachers and other educational staff,
- and many other tasks.

These unique responsibilities have the potential to add stress to an already high-pressure profession, which is exactly why educators need enhanced emotional resilience. Not to mention, when teachers fail to effectively do their jobs, they can expect to be swiftly held accountable. Whether they are being held accountable by department chairs, principals, or parents, teachers will most definitely be challenged to do more and do better. These factors certainly will challenge the emotional resilience and resolve of any teacher.

Conclusion: Summarizing "Resilience"

According to researchers from Pennsylvania State University, resilient teachers are much more likely to successfully handle the management, instructional, and emotional challenges of the classroom.[xix] They also believe teachers who lack this trait are more susceptible to high levels of distress that can lead to burnout.[xx] For this reason, they suggest providing teachers with specialized professional development to address the social and

"An opportunity to demonstrate resilience is usually dressed up as a problem or a disappointment."
— Jahkari Taylor

emotional well-being of teachers.[xxi] I believe research speaks to the need to help teachers develop emotional resilience. As researchers continue to investigate teacher stress and teacher burnout, I believe specialized emotional training will eventually have to move to the forefront of the discussion about teacher effectiveness. In addition, teacher preparation programs and school divisions will have to proactively address the need to develop a teacher's social and emotional competence by providing supports that can help teachers practice stress reduction techniques.

Here are ten practical tips for decreasing educator stress:

1. Reduce how much television you watch.
2. Research "Mindfulness in Education."
3. Pray and/or meditate weekly, if not daily.
4. Listen to calming music.
5. Exercise or go for a relaxing walk.
6. Journal weekly, if not daily. *Writing has been proven to ease stress and anxiety!*
7. Read inspiring and empowering literature.
8. Make room for quality relationships – No toxic people!
9. Limit how much teacher work you do when you are off the clock.

10. Attend conferences and workshops that enhance your ability to teach.

Suggested Journal: *Overcoming Burnout Daily Journal: 100 Opportunities to Change Your Own Mind*

Reflection, Response, and Affirmation
Trait #4 - "Resilience"

"Resilient" with Students

- *Be honest with yourself:* How well do you handle stress?
- Have you ever had to demonstrate resilience in your classroom? (Tweet your response to @purposepushers using the hashtag #ImResilient.)

"Resilient" with Adults

- If your colleagues could choose one of the following to describe you, which one would they choose: 1) Sunshine – Radiates positivity 2) Present and functioning 3) Always complaining 4) Completely burnt out.

Affirmation: "I am a Teacher with a Purpose"

- "Today, I will be more in tune with my own emotions. If I experience disappointment or frustration, I will recover and be better than before."

A group of students from Arkansas identified "a lack of encouragement" as the biggest problem in society today."[xxii] These young people were so moved by compassion to do something about this issue that they launched a national day of

"A word of encouragement from a teacher to a child can change a life. A word of encouragement from a spouse can save a marriage. A word of encouragement from a leader can inspire a person to reach her potential."
— *John C. Maxwell*

encouragement to empower people to confront discouragement through words and acts of inspiration and support.[xxiii] In June 2007, this student-led group of high schoolers attended a leadership camp at Harding University in Searcy, Arkansas, where they eventually conceptualized this day. Since then, The National Day of Encouragement has been picking up momentum. It has since been endorsed by President George W. Bush and his father, George H. W. Bush.

Although these students could have easily acknowledged a different issue as the biggest problem in society today, many would agree that our world lacks encouragement. Think about it… Where would you direct a person to go if they are looking to be encouraged? Sadly, most people will draw a blank if asked this question. Although we would love to believe school should come to mind as a place where one can go to receive encouragement, this is not always the case for students or teachers. While most teachers may not cite a lack of encouragement as the biggest problem in society, they may agree that a lack of encouragement is one of the biggest problems in their profession.

What does the research say?

Kim Inyoung and William Loadman (1998) of The Ohio State University conducted a study on factors that predict teacher job satisfaction. Among the many factors that contribute to or detract from teacher job satisfaction, they noted teacher job satisfaction is very much influenced by interpersonal relationships in the school context.[xxiv] They alluded to the fact that teachers' relationships with colleagues, their sense of collaboration and community among staff, and whether they experience recognition from other teachers will influence their ability to feel a sense of job satisfaction.[xxv] Teachers want to be recognized by the teachers they work with as well as the educational leaders they work under. According to Tamara Sober and Jesse Senechal (2017), "Teachers experienced higher job

67

satisfaction when principals built trusting relationships and communicated positively with teachers."[xxvi] Even on an international level, the lack of encouragement and support is contributing to the dissatisfaction of teachers worldwide. One recent study of educators in Pakistan also confirmed the fact that interpersonal relationships contribute to the satisfaction or dissatisfaction of educators.[xxvii]

As indicated by the research, teachers desire and expect to develop quality relationships on their jobs. They expect to be acknowledged, not ignored. They expect to be encouraged, not discouraged. This is exactly why Teachers with a Purpose must possess the trait of encouragement. By possessing this trait, teachers can contribute to a healthier, more encouraging work environment for students and staff. When teachers become intentional about using encouragement as a tool to inspire others, the overall school culture will benefit tremendously. This means teachers will become more satisfied, more motivated, and more productive on their jobs. Usually, more satisfaction, more motivation, and more production translate to increased student achievement.

According to the Oxford dictionary, encouragement is "the act of giving someone support, confidence, or hope." A good analogy for providing encouragement is "cheerleading." Cheerleaders can be found at almost every sporting event, cheering their team on to victory. They seem to always have a smile on their face as they attempt to give support, confidence, and hope. As noted in earlier chapters, educators work in a highly demanding and pressured environment. On any given day, the average educator is starving for someone to give them some support, confidence, and hope. In most cases, they just want someone to acknowledge their efforts, or as a former colleague expressed to me, "sometimes I just need an 'attaboy.'" Undoubtedly, educators need cheerleaders.

Although many educators would love to come to work and hear encouraging words of support and affirmation, many believe they are more likely to hear negative words of complaint and criticism, particularly in teacher workrooms. There was a time when teacher workrooms were solely used to grade papers, submit grades, contact parents, and discuss how to be more effective in the classroom. Yet, many educators would agree that they are starting to become synonymous with "spaces reserved for murmuring, complaining, and sharing the latest gossip in the building." When I was pursuing my undergraduate degree, one of my teacher preparation professors warned my entire class to avoid the teacher workroom at all costs. She said, "As often as you can, grade papers and get your work done in your classroom during your planning time because teacher workrooms are unprofessional toxic spaces." We all had no clue what she was talking about because we did not have a reference point at the time.

Give and Receive Encouragement

Over a decade later, having worked in numerous schools from the primary to the secondary level, I have to say my professor was trying to give us wise advice in advance. In a nutshell, she was trying to get us to distance ourselves from people and spaces in the school setting that could cause us to be discouraged. Throughout my career, I have personally heard teachers demean students, belittle parents, and conspire to rebel against their principals in the teacher workroom. On a few occasions, I have heard explosive arguments between teachers that I thought would turn into a full-blown Ultimate Fighting Championship bout.

This is not to say teacher workrooms are the problem. They just happen to be spaces where people relax and speak without filters. I share these personal stories to provoke honest reflection about where we are as an educational system so we can chart the path forward. There is much progress to be made in terms of creating spaces of encouragement. No educator can afford to give room to discouragement because it is contagious. It has to be avoided at all costs. Although small voices of discouragement may percolate through the halls of schools today, I believe we have the collective power to create spaces of encouragement in every school. If everyone in the school system will commit to giving and receiving encouragement, schools can become institutions of transformation. This will certainly require a change of mindset, a plan of action, and intentional efforts on the part of everyone inside of the school. Transforming the school into an encouraging place is not impossible to accomplish. Together, educators can create a healthy school culture where teachers are satisfied, and students are achieving to their potential. If we are to make this happen, learning to give and receive encouragement will have to be an integral part of the process.

Here are two practical things schools can do to develop Teachers with a Purpose who possess the invaluable trait of encouragement:

1. **Create affinity groups or "Support Circles."**

A "Support Circle" is a specially designed group of diverse individuals who are committed to supporting and intentionally encouraging one another. Each circle provides opportunities for staff to establish healthy working relationships in a shared environment where a sense of connectedness and belonging can be fostered. (For more details about how to develop support circles in your building, order a copy of *Support Circles: A guide to boost teacher morale in 20 minutes or less.*)

2. **Develop school-wide matrices that employ "common encouraging language."**

For example, "Speak Life," "Speak Encouragement," and/or "Speak Professionally" should become common phrases in professional learning communities, teams, teacher workrooms, and/or classrooms. Matrices of this kind can help delineate professional boundaries in the school. This is essential for developing an encouraging school culture.

Conclusion: Summarizing "Encouragement"

Life is very similar to the most exhilarating roller coaster ride. It is jampacked with twists, turns, exhilarating highs, and nauseating lows. Therefore, everyone requires a dose of intentional encouragement every now and again. While most people ride roller coasters on special occasions, teachers seem to take a ride every day. Every day teachers enter the classroom is another day to go high or to go low, to experience a twist or a turn. For these reasons, educators need to be encouraged daily. The question is, who should be required to provide the daily encouragement? I personally believe educators must provide the encouragement for one another. No one has a true understanding of the highs and lows of being a teacher like a teacher, which is why I believe teachers must intentionally encourage one another. At the end of the day, educators need each other. As Teachers with a Purpose, we must be cognizant of the need for encouragement in the field of education. We must strive to be intentional about encouraging teachers as well as students.

> "If we're going to bring out the best in people, we, too, need to sow seeds of encouragement."
> — Joel Osteen

Reflection, Response, and Affirmation
Trait #5 - "Encouragement"

"Encouragement" with Students

- *Be honest with yourself:* Do you criticize, and discipline students more than you encourage them? *(Start practicing PBIS consistently!)*
- What can you do in your classroom to encourage your students daily? (Tweet your response to @purposepushers using the hashtag #Encouragement.)

"Encouragement" with Adults

- When was the last time you were encouraged by one of your colleagues? How did it make you feel?
- When was the last time you encouraged one of your colleagues?
- Have you ever encouraged your principal? If not, please do so as soon as possible. They need it, too!

Affirmation: "I am a Teacher with a Purpose"

- "Today, I will do my part to create a more encouraging environment in my school. I will intentionally encourage students and staff."

Although "hope" and "optimism" are closely related, they are not identical. According to Allie Grasgreen (2012), *optimism* is "the belief that good things will

"Hope is being able to see that there is light despite of all the darkness."
— Desmond Tutu

happen," while *hope* "deals with whether one can find a way to make good things happen."[xxviii] According to Rick Snyder (1995), a clinical psychologist and the foremost pioneer of hope research, hope is "the process of thinking about one's goals, along with the motivation to move toward those goals (agency), and the ways to achieve those goals (pathways)."[xxix] For the sake of comparison, hope is much more action-oriented than optimism. While optimistic people *believe* the state of education can change, hopeful people are willing to *act* to bring about that change. With an educational system riddled with many deflating issues such as inadequate pay, large class sizes, and unmotivated students, we certainly would benefit from interjecting hope into schools.

In Portugal, some researchers studied the impact of boosting "hope" in middle school students. Their longitudinal study showed long-term gains in life satisfaction and mental health from boosting hope.[xxx] One researcher noted they were able to boost hope by training students "to visualize their goals, to see how they'll achieve them, even when obstacles arise."[xxxi] Portugal is not the only place starting to take a deeper look at "hope" and its impact on achievement and effort. American researchers conducted a study on 213 college freshmen to evaluate the impact "hope" may have on adults.[xxxii] Students were administered the "Hope Scale" survey to evaluate their level of hopefulness. Students who were deemed to have "high hopes" ended up with higher GPAs and were more likely to graduate from college than those who were considered to have "low hopes." The results of the study indicated that hope was a predictor of academic success, motivation, and perseverance.

Teachers Need Hope

Over the last two decades, there has been extensive research on "hope" and its ability to enhance a person's self-efficacy, motivation, and general well-being.[xxxiii] Yet, there has been relatively no studies on hope's impact on educators. As mentioned earlier, teacher burnout is a real threat in the field of education, but many educational leaders do not even want to utter the words *teacher burnout*. As an instructional coach, my question to educational leaders has always been, *how can uninspired teachers be expected to inspire students*? To expect someone who has low hopes to somehow motivate others is illogical and unfair, to say the least. Therefore, I believe educational leaders need to put forth much more of a concerted effort to inspire teachers while helping them develop a sense of hopefulness.

Hopeful "Teachers with A Purpose"

Teachers with a Purpose are not genetically born with a personality that allows them to always remain calm and cool. They are not inherently more hopeful than others; they simply choose to maintain their optimism and hopefulness despite the pressures and stressors that accompany the profession. They understand that school is emotionally taxing for students and staff, which is exactly why they intentionally strive to exude a sense of confident hope. They have no other choice but to expect things to improve over time. Therefore, they embrace the responsibility of modeling hope for students and staff. They do not model hope because of wishful thinking; they model hope because they know it is essential to their own emotional and psychological well-being. While some teachers may try to treat "hope" like a switch that can be turned on or off at their disposal, "Teachers with a Purpose" understand that maintaining hopefulness is not only necessary to serve students but also to maintain peace, joy, and emotional stability.

Here are some things teachers can do to overcome their hopelessness and help students overcome it as well:

For the Teacher

1. Research success stories of low-performing schools that turned into institutions where all students had an opportunity to achieve success.
2. Listen to motivational speakers.
3. Attend inspiring educational conferences and workshops to receive professional development continuously.

For the Student

1. Find articles of individuals who overcame tremendous odds to achieve personal success and incorporate it into a lesson or class discussion.

2. Find a brief motivational video to watch with students. Have students take notes on the video and/or engage in a Think-Pair-Share about the video.

3. Give students an opportunity to express their dreams.

Conclusion: Summarizing "Hopefulness"

Hopefulness, as defined as "the belief that one can find a way to make good things happen," is very similar to the concept of "teacher efficacy." According to Tschannen-Moran and Hoy (2001), teacher efficacy refers to a teacher's "judgment of his or her capabilities to bring

"Making a difference begins with believing in yourself. If you don't believe you can be a difference maker, you will never give yourself a chance to make a difference."
– Jahkari Taylor

about desired outcomes of student engagement and learning, even among those students who may be difficult or unmotivated."[xxxiv] In other words, teacher efficacy is what goes on in the mind of every educator in terms of how they view their chances of making a difference in the lives of learners. Teachers with high levels of teacher efficacy tend to be more hopeful. They often believe they can reach the most seemingly unreachable learners. However, teachers with low levels of teacher efficacy tend to demonstrate a "fixed mindset" as opposed to a "growth mindset."[xxxv] They often feel as if some learners cannot be reached, no matter how much a teacher tries to reach them. They tend to think a student's home environment, cultural background, socioeconomic status, or other external factors that are out of the control of the teacher make reaching students impossible. These teachers have pretty much lost hope or are in the process of losing it.

This is exactly why Teachers with a Purpose must always maintain their hopefulness. A high level of hopefulness is likely to translate to a high level of teacher efficacy. Research suggests that the collective efficacy of teachers can be a stronger predictor of student achievement than factors such as parental involvement, home environment, and socioeconomic status (Donohoo, Hattie, and Eells, 2018, p.44).[xxxvi] In other words, teachers have the power to combat the negative influences and *invisible baggage* that can potentially hinder student achievement. If Teachers with a Purpose maintain hope and persevere in the belief that they can make a difference, all students will have a chance to succeed.

Reflection, Response, and Affirmation
Trait #6 - "Hopefulness"

"Hopefulness" with Students

- Have you ever intentionally attempted to give your students hope?
- List one way that you can help your students become more hopeful about their academic future. (Tweet your response to @purposepushers using the hashtag #GiveHope.)

"Hopefulness" with Adults

- What is the main cause of teachers losing hope?
- How can school leaders help create a more hopeful environment for faculty and staff?

(Tweet your response to @purposepushers using the hashtag #HopefulSchools.)

Affirmation: "I am a Teacher with a Purpose"

- "Today, I will look for the best in every situation, and I will model a hopeful attitude for my students and my colleagues."

Trait #7 - "Relational"

Teaching is a profession driven by relationships. Whether it be relationships with students, staff, parents, and other community stakeholders, relationships must be front, center, and top priority. When relationships are neglected or

"Relational teaching is an educational philosophy that is built on fostering an atmosphere of love in the learning environment, where every student feels capable, connected, and cared for."
— Jahkari Taylor

undermined, students and teachers both tend to underperform. This obviously cannot be the case if schools are to become high-achieving institutions that develop the next generation of leaders. Therefore, I believe the goal of every school must be to adopt an educational philosophy that encourages and prioritizes relationships over everything else.

What does the research say?

According to the National Association of Secondary School Principals (NASSP), "A thorough understanding of where a student is coming from is often difficult to reach, yet a school culture that systematically encourages that understanding will make great strides in helping students learn." (NASSP, 2011, p. 2)[xxxvii] It is not sufficient for individuals within a school to embrace a "relationship-first" mindset. The entire school must intentionally seek to create a school-wide culture that supports a "relationship-first" mindset. This means educational leaders and educators must ensure that all students feel as if they have at least one person in the building whom they can trust and talk to. There should be no students who feel anonymous, marginalized, or disconnected from the whole. To make sure students feel connected, educators must first seek to get to know their students.

When educators take the initiative to learn about their students, they show students that they care about them on a personal level and not just on an academic level. There is an extensive amount of research that alludes to student-teacher relationships as the key to increasing student achievement while reducing disruptive and undesirable behaviors in the classroom. Kohn (1996) states, "Children are more likely to be respectful when important adults in their lives respect them. They are more likely to care about others if they know they are cared about."[xxxviii] Marzano (2003) asserts that "students will resist rules and procedures along with the consequent disciplinary actions if the foundation of a good relationship is lacking."[xxxix]

Not only is creating a relationship-driven culture in school, the key to student achievement, and classroom management, but it is also the key to student motivation. According to Wentzel (1997), "students are more motivated by teachers whom they perceive as caring."[xl] If you ask teachers from across the nation, which type of students are the most difficult to work with, many of them will say "unmotivated students." Unlike students who demonstrate problematic behaviors, unmotivated students are the most unengaged. While students who demonstrate disruptive behaviors may be unengaged for a day or two, unmotivated students may be unengaged for weeks. They often arrive to school unprepared and treat their desk like a comfortable queen size bed. They are more likely to put their heads on their desks and fall asleep, as opposed to participating in the daily lesson. These students will not stand a chance of succeeding in school if educators are unwilling to build a relationship with them.

All students can benefit from an educator's willingness to build a relationship with them. Whether students are unmotivated, gifted, or impoverished, they need teachers who are relational. Haberman (1999) states, "the ability of teachers to forge relationships with children in poverty and connect with them is the key factor in high-performing schools" (The Center for Public Education).[xli] In terms of academic achievement, building positive relationships with students has been proven to improve students' academic performance and educational outcomes. According to Topor (2010), "the quality of the student-teacher relationship was significantly related to the child's academic performance, measured by both standardized achievement test scores and the child's classroom academic performance."[xlii] The research is clear: schools need to help teachers become "relationship-oriented." Here are three practical things teachers can do to develop a relational mindset:

1. Research and read literature about the significance of building rapport with students.

2. Attend professional development that provides strategies for rapport building in the classroom context.

3. Take a moment to recall the educators throughout your personal life who have inspired you. Nine times out of ten, these were educators who prioritized relationships first, and made you feel capable, connected, and cared for.

For most children, teachers will easily become some of the most influential people in their lives. This is because students spend a large portion of their lives in the presence of educators. Most students attend school for around 7 hours per day, 180 days per year. When you multiply these numbers throughout a student's life from primary school to high school, the average student is guaranteed to spend over 16,000 hours with teachers. This is a lot of time to be influenced.

Through the bond students develop with their teachers, they pick up on mannerisms, gestures, values, and essential character traits. Therefore, one can make the argument that teachers are the most influential people in the lives of children outside of the influence of their parents. This is why all teachers must strive to become Teachers with a Purpose. This means teachers must be intentional about how they use their influence to mold the next generation. Students can learn the value of hard work, dedication, and commitment from their teachers if teachers are intentional enough. Students can learn to value people and appreciate diversity through the relationships they develop with their teachers. For this reason, every school needs Teachers with a Purpose. Families require it, communities need it, and our world depends on it. Every educator must consciously strive to become a relational Teachers with a Purpose.

Conclusion: Summarizing "Relational"

Relationships are what drives learning. Not the curriculum, the content, or the assessments. Not the technology or the teaching techniques. Students learn naturally in the context of relationships. Therefore,

"No significant learning can occur without a significant relationship."
— Dr. James Comer

relationships should not be second to anything in the field of education. As students develop a sense of connection with their teachers, trust can be established. Once this occurs, classroom disruptions decrease, student motivation increases, and academic achievement for all students becomes a realistic goal. As noted throughout this chapter, the research in support of *Relational Teaching* abounds. If you ever need to be reminded of the significance of building rapport with students, I encourage you to view Rita Pierson's 7-minute video on *Ted.com* titled, "Every Kid Needs a Champion." It will inspire you to become a relational Teachers with a Purpose.

Reflection, Response, and Affirmation
Trait #7 - "Relational"

"Relational" with Students

- *Be honest with yourself:* Do you prioritize relationships over content and curriculum?
- What strategies/activities do you use to build rapport with students? (Tweet your response to @purposepushers using the hashtag #Relational.)

Suggested reading: Relational Teaching: Connection is the Key!

"Relational" with Adults

- Are you relational with your colleagues? Do you seek to develop quality relationships with your coworkers?
- On a scale from 1 (needs improvement) to 10 (I am a master collaborator), rate your ability to collaborate with adults?
- If a relationship with another colleague gets off to a rocky start, what would you do to restore the relationship?

- "Today, I will be intentional with my attempts to connect with my students and co-workers.

No one ever arrives, and all true Teachers with a Purpose will agree with this sentiment. This is because Teachers with a Purpose are individuals who are always in pursuit of personal and professional development. They

"Never give up and be confident in what you do. There may be tough times, but the difficulties which you face will make you more determined to achieve your objectives and to win against all the odds."
— Marta

are the type of people who curiously look forward to attending conferences, workshops, and in-services. They are the type of employees who enjoy reading books and articles that contain the latest research on trends in education. They are not boring bookworms; they are simply focused on being the best they can be in a profession that has the power to change the world. They understand that there is too much at stake to be a mediocre educator; therefore, they continually strive for self-improvement.

To be clear, Teachers with a Purpose are not individuals who sit on top of the educational apex, disdainfully looking down on "rookies." They are humble helpers of all they encounter. This is why students, parents, colleagues, and principals enjoy their company. They genuinely want everyone to succeed at a high level, and they are willing to do what they can to help others. That's why they are loved, respected, and are highly sought after. It's not just their expertise in the field; it's their character. It's who they are in and outside of work.

As I iterated in the opening chapter, Teachers with a Purpose are rare. Yet, the reality is the educational system cannot afford for this to be the case. Every school should be saturated with Teachers with a Purpose. Every student should be constantly passed from one Teacher with a Purpose to the next. When this happens, schools will become institutions of transformation.

Only then will all students have equitable opportunities to thrive and demonstrate growth. Whether students are White, Black, Hispanic, poor, or privileged, they are in desperate need of adults who will believe in them when they don't believe in themselves. They need people who can demonstrate instructional competence as well as emotional empathy. They need teachers who deliver quality instruction while modeling quality character. They need Teachers with a Purpose! Let's make it our personal mission to continue to develop ourselves and those around us, so we can ensure that every student has access to life-changing *"Teachers with a Purpose!"*

Reflection, Response, and Affirmation
"Striving to be a "Teacher with a Purpose"

"I am Striving"

- *"I will strive to be the best educator I can be. This means I will invest in my professional development and my personal growth so that my character aligns with the great calling of being an educator. I will seek to make a positive impact on students, staff, and the community in which I serve. I am a Teacher with a Purpose!"*

Daily Affirmation:

"I declare that I am a Teacher with a Purpose!"

Meet the Author

Mr. Jahkari "JT" Taylor is a husband, father, mentor, and senior pastor at The Focus Church. He has earned a Bachelor of Science degree from Norfolk State University, a Master of Education degree from Liberty University, and a Master of Arts degree in Theology from Liberty Baptist Theological Seminary. He is also the author of *Relational Teaching, Overcoming Burnout, True Leaders LEAD,* and *Becoming One Flesh.* He currently works as a Title 1 Instructional Coach.

He is also the president and CEO of Purpose Pushers LLC., which is a hybrid educational consulting company that couples motivational speaking with research-based professional development. Through Purpose Pushers LLC, JT aims to develop and inspire talent while helping educational leaders, educators, and students find passion and purpose. He provides direct consultations, instructional coaching, interactive research-based workshops, professional development, keynote speeches, school assemblies, and much more. JT Taylor is most certainly a visionary leader and a Purpose Pusher.

For speaking engagements or professional developments, please contact JT Taylor at jtwithapurpose@gmail.com or visit www.purposepushers.com.

References

[i] Cawelti, G. (Ed.). (2004). Handbook of research on improving student achievement (2nd ed.). Arlington, VA: Educational Research Service. Stronge, J. H., Tucker, P. D., & Hindman, J. L. (2004). *Handbook for qualities of effective teachers*. Alexandria, VA: Association for Supervision & Curriculum Development.

[ii] Jefferson to Cabell, December 25, 1820, Special Collections, University of Virginia Library. Transcription available at Founders Online.

[iii] Generations in America. "Generations at a glance." http://re-generations.org/generations-in-america/

[iv] Generational Differences Chart. http://www.wmfc.org/uploads/GenerationalDifferencesChart.pdf

[v] Jessica L. Semega, Kayla R. Fontenot, and Melissa A. Kollar for the U.S. Census Bureau, "Income and Poverty in the United States: 2016" (United States Department of Commerce, 2017), available at https://www.census.gov/content/dam/Census/library/publications/2017/demo/P60-259.pdf

[vi] Thomas, Brandi (2016) "How Living in Poverty Affects Children's Brain Development." Retrieved from https://today.duke.edu/2016/10/how-living-poverty-affects-children's-brain-development on June 21, 2018.

[viivii] Ibid.

[viii] Ibid.

[ix] Sleek, Scott (2015). "How Poverty Affects the Brain and Behavior." Retrieved from https://www.psychologicalscience.org/observer/how-poverty-affects-the-brain-and-behavior

[x] The Understood Team. "3 Arras of Executive Functioning." Retrieved from https://www.understood.org/en/learning-attention-issues/child-learning-disabilities/executive-functioning-issues/3-areas-of-executive-function on June 21, 2018.

[xi] Stone, Michael. (2002). Forgiveness in the workplace. *Industrial and Commercial Training*, 34(7), 278-286.

[xii] Jones, Sandra (2016). "I don't deserve it!' Taunted teacher storms out of Richmond class" https://wtvr.com/2016/10/07/frustrated-richmond-classroom/

[xiii] Scelfo, Julie. (2016). "Angela Duckworth on passion, grit and success." *New York Times*. April 8, 2016 retrieved on June 30, 2018. https://www.nytimes.com/2016/04/10/education/edlife/passion-grit-success.html

[xiv] Rees Clare S., Breen Lauren J., Cusack Lynette, Hegney Desley (2015). Understanding individual resilience in the workplace: the international collaboration of workforce resilience model. *Frontiers in Psychology*. Vol 6(73). https://www.frontiersin.org/article/10.3389/fpsyg.2015.00073fff

[xv] Beehr, T. A. and Newman, J. E. (1978), Job Stress, Employee Health, and Organizational Effectiveness: A Facet Analysis, Model, and Literature Review. *Personnel Psychology*, 31: 665-699.

[xvi] Fruedenberger, H. (1974). Staff burnout. *Journal of Social Issues*, 30, 159–165.

[xvii] Ibid.

[xviii] Williams, C. S. (2011). "Combatting Teacher Burnout." *The Journal* (Technological Horizons in Education) 38, 10. Retrieved from https://thejournal.com/articles/2011/11/03/teacher-burnout.aspx

[xix] Jennings, P., Snowberg, K., Coccia, M., & Greenberg, M. (2011). Improving Classroom Learning Environments by Cultivating Awareness and Resilience in Education (CARE): Results of Two Pilot Studies. *The Journal of Classroom Interaction, 46*(1), 37-48. Retrieved from http://www.jstor.org/stable/23870550.

[xx] Ibid.

[xxi] Ibid.

[xxii] Good News Network. (2008) ."National Day of Encouragement – September 12." Retrieved from https://www.goodnewsnetwork.org/day-of-encouragement/

[xxiii] Ibid.

[xxiv] Kim, I., & Loadman, W. (1994). Predicting teacher job satisfaction. (ERIC Document Reproduction Service No. ED 383 707).

[xxv] Ibid.

[xxvi] Tamara Sober & Jesse Senechal. (2017), "Atmospheric Change." Published in the *Virginia Journal of Education*. Virginia Education Association, p.10. April 2017. Retrieved from http://www.veanea.org/home/2854.htm

[xxvii] Sahito, Z. & Vaisanen, P. (2016). Dimensions of Job satisfaction of Teacher Educators: A Qualitative Study of the Universities of Sindh Province of Pakistan. Journal of Curriculum and Teaching, 5(2), 43-54. https://doi.org/10.5430/jct.v5n2p43

[xxviii] Grasgreen, Allie (2012) "Here's Hoping" *Inside Higher Ed.* Retrieved from https://www.insidehighered.com/news/2012/07/06/researchers-apply-hope-theory-boost-college-student-success

[xxix] Snyder, C. R. (1995). Conceptualizing, measuring, and nurturing hope. *Journal of Counseling and Development*, 73, 355–360.

[xxx] Marques, S. C., Lopez, S. J., & Pais-Ribeiro, J. L. (2011a). Building hope for the future: A program to foster strengths in middle-school students. *Journal of Happiness Studies, 12*, 139–152.

[xxxi] Ibid.

[xxxii] R. Snyder, C & Shorey, Hal & Cheavens, Jennifer & Pulvers, Kim & H. Adams III, Virgil & Wiklund, Cynthia. (2002). Hope and academic success in college. *Journal of Educational Psychology*. 94. 820-826. 10.1037/0022-0663.94.4.820.

[xxxiii] Magaletta, P. R., & Oliver, J. M. (1999). The hope construct, will and ways: Their relative relations with self-efficacy, optimism, and general well-being. Journal of Clinical Psychology, 55, 539–551.

[xxxiv] Tschannen-Moran, Megan and Anita Woolfolk Hoy, "Teacher efficacy: capturing an elusive construct." *Teaching and Teacher Education*, Volume 17, Issue 7, 2001, Pages 783-805, ISSN 0742-051X, https://doi.org/10.1016/S0742-051X(01)00036-1.

[xxxv] Brock, A., & Hundley, H. (2016). *The growth mindset coach: A teacher's month-by-month handbook for empowering students to achieve*. Berkeley, CA: Ulysses Press.

[xxxvi] Donohoo, Jenni, Hattie, John, and Eells, Rachel (2018). "The power of collective efficacy." ASCD. Leading the Energized School 75(6), 40-44.

[xxxvii] NASSP. (2011) "The breaking ranks framework: An overview. p.2 http://media.collegeboard.com/digitalServices/pdf/advocacy/M8R4_BR framework_pp1-6.pdf

[xxxviii] Kohn, A. (1996). Beyond discipline: From compliance to community. Alexandria, Va: ASCD, 111.

[xxxix] Marzano, R. J. (with Marzano, J. S., & Pickering, D. J.). (2003b). Classroom management that works. Alexandria, VA: ASCD.

[xl] Wentzel, K. R. (1997). Student motivation in middle school: The role of perceived pedagogical caring. *Journal of Educational Psychology*, 89(3), 411-419.

[xli] The Center for Public Education (1999). "High-performing, High-poverty schools: Research review."

[xlii] Topor, D. R., Keane, S. P., Shelton, T. L., & Calkins, S. D. (2010). Parent involvement and student academic performance: A multiple mediational analysis. *Journal of Prevention & Intervention in the Community*, *38*(3), 183–197. http://doi.org/10.1080/10852352.2010.486297

Made in the USA
Monee, IL
15 October 2023

44623631R00057